Baseball

Records

Update

1993

Edited by Lyle Spatz

Prepared by the Records Committee of The Society for American Baseball Research

Published by The Society for American Baseball Research

P.O. Box 93183

Cleveland, OH 44101

Designed by Jeanne Criscola/Criscola Design

Printed and manufactured in the United States of America

by EBSCO Media

Birmingham, Alabama

Baseball Records Update 1993

Contents

Introduction

The SABR Records Committee was formed by the SABR Board of Directors in 1975, and given the mandate "to establish an accurate set of records for organized baseball". This is the first in a series of publications designed to fulfill that mandate.

Over the years, researchers have uncovered many errors and inconsistencies in baseball's historical record. These errors are of two major types: (1) those errors that deal with accomplishments, positive or negative, that have been accepted as major league or individual league records: the most, the highest, the fewest, the lowest, etc., or (2) errors in the yearly and lifetime records of an individual, or a team.

Also during this time, researchers have been working to fill in data for statistical categories that heretofore had not been recorded, especially for the earlier periods of baseball history. Some examples of these are batter hit-by-pitch, wild pitches, and passed balls.

The majority of people doing these kinds of research have been SABR members, many of them members of SABR's Records Committee. Through the committee newsletter, the SABR newsletter, and personal correspondence, committee members have tried to share and disseminate as much of this material as possible. Yet many of us believe that we are not reaching nearly enough people. It is only by happenstance that the information is being communicated to the whole of the SABR membership. This publication is an attempt to reach both that membership and those interested baseball fans who are not SABR members. Additionally, we hope that the publishers of the various record books and encyclopedias, and the baseball "establishment", persuaded by the evidence we present, will correct the errors and omissions we document.

For the overwhelming mass of individual, team, and league statistics, these publications are in agreement and are correct. However, baseball's record-keeping has not always been so meticulous as

it is today. This is particularly true in the game's early years. There are numerous cases of omissions, transpositions, double-counting, addition errors, and what can best be described as illegibility. These are errors that occurred at the original source (in the accounting of individual games), or in the league's accounting at year's end. For much of this early period, individual totals and league totals were not necessarily compared to see that they balanced. These "official sheets" date from 1903 for the National League, and from 1905 for the American League. Of course not all statistical categories, for games or for players, were kept from those beginning years. Runs batted in, earned run average, batter strikeouts, and saves are just some examples of statistical categories that were added to the official sheets at later dates.

Other mistakes have come about as a result of the work done in the compilation of the encyclopedias and record books, some as a result of putting together the Information Concepts Corporation (ICI) data in the 1960's. ICI data were collected for those years and categories for which official sheets were not available, and together with those official sheets formed the data base for the encyclopedias. Assembling these volumes is such an enormous undertaking, that it is not surprising that errors occur. This is in no way a criticism of those responsible for these publications; that there are so few errors is to their everlasting credit. I can not emphasize that strongly enough. Those of us who do baseball research understand how great a debt we owe them.

The players affected by the changes that we have made range from fringe players to Hall-of-Famers. In some cases we have dealt with icons of the game, men such as Walter Johnson, Tris Speaker, and Lou Gehrig. Their accomplishments are legendary, and certain numbers associated with them are so imbedded in the memory of baseball fans that some think it sacrilegious to alter them. Those of us who attempt to do so are accused of being "fanatical crusaders," more obsessed with statistics than with the "romance" of the game. Nothing could be further from the truth. Each person who has contributed to this study has loved the game since childhood and continues to do so. It is inconceivable that anyone who didn't love baseball would devote as much time to studying it as we do. But as Aristotle said of his mentor, "Plato is dear to me, but dearer still is truth." That is basically what we are, seekers of truth; not for the purpose of inflating or deflating the accomplishments of one player at the expense of another, but to ensure that each player's accomplishments are accounted for as accurately as possible. We hope, with this paper and future ones, to move the "historical record" in that direction. Knowing that there are many more inaccuracies yet to be discovered, even perhaps for the players included in this report, we consider these corrections to be only a beginning.

Thus, the purpose of this publication is not one of revolution, but rather of evolution. We want to make the historic record a little more accurate, and a little more consistent. Several of the corrections that appear here have already been changed in one or more of the record books and encyclopedias; others have been acknowledged and will appear in future editions. That is not meant as an endorsement of one publication over another. I know of no serious researcher who does not make use of multiple sources. Rather it is our obligation to make the case for each proposed change sufficiently convincing that each of the record books and encyclopedias will accept it on merit. As the great English philosopher

John Locke said, "It is one thing to show a man that he is in error, and another to put him in possesion of the truth."

The people responsible for the research in this publication have devoted a great deal of time to their respective subjects. They have pored over old newspapers, guides, official records, and ICI records. They have looked at miles of microfilm, from a variety of sources, searching through box scores and comparing game accounts. In all cases, they adhered to the scoring rules and customs of the day. As previously stated, only in very few cases did they find what seemed to be a demonstrable error. We believe that the instances cited in this paper are not matters of interpretation, but are clearly errors.

We contend, for example, that Walter Johnson won 33 games in 1912, not 32; that in his career he won 417 games and not 416. We believe that the evidence supporting this contention is so compelling that to disregard it would be damaging to the historical integrity of the game. We fail to see how clinging to a number that is obviously wrong adds to the "romance" of the game, or how accepting a correct one detracts from it. Even if we had discovered that Johnson had won "only" 415 games, could that possibly alter anyone's opinion of his greatness, or his place in history?

Therefore we offer these corrections and reconciliations in a spirit of collegiality and cooperation. We trust that they will be received in the same way. Our only goal is to contribute to a more accurate set of records for organized baseball.

Acknowledgements

As in all publications such as this, it is the product of the efforts of many people. From its inception, the concept and writing of this Records Committee publication has had the full support and encouragement of SABR president, **Lloyd Johnson**, and SABR executive director, **Morris Eckhouse**. Publications director, **Mark Alvarez**, also has lent much support, in addition to being a most gentle editor and understanding schedule-maker.

But of course, the vast majority of credit goes to those members of the Records Committee who submitted the entries that make up this volume. They are the ones who discovered the errors and inconsistencies that are corrected here. Whether it be **Frank Williams** and **Joe Dittmar**, who submitted multiple entries, or someone who just double-checked and confirmed some fact, all baseball fans owe each of them a debt of gratitude.

The nature of this type of research requires, in most cases, a great deal of cooperation and mutual assistance. Ideas, information, news accounts and box-scores are continually being exchanged. With that in mind, and with the fervent hope that no one who helped in even the slightest way is omitted, here are the contributors.

The corrections to the records of Dick Rudolph, Cy Young, Hugh Duffy, Tris Speaker, Herman Long, Walter Johnson, Bob Groom, Chick Stahl, Roger Connor, Hardy Richardson, Harry Stovey, and Dan Brouthers were submitted by **Frank Williams**. Those who helped Frank with one or more of the above players include **Bob Davids, Bill Deane, Paul Doherty, Cliff Kachline, Don Luce, Pete Palmer**, the late **Keith Sutton, John Schwartz, Seymour Siwoff, Henry Thomas, Bob Tiemann, Ed Walton, Joe Wayman**, and the late **G.E. Righter**.

The corrections to the records of Bobby Lowe and Mike Tiernan were submitted by **Pete Palmer**. Pete also helped **Bob Davids** and **Ray Gonzalez**, who submitted the entry on Lou Gehrig. Pete also discovered the errors in the records of the other 1926 Yankees.

David Stephan and **Bill Deane** were responsible for the entry concerning the one game switch of the batting records of Eddie Collins and Buck Weaver. They were helped by **Ron Rakowski**.

Joe Wayman, whose corrections to Jack Chesbro's lifetime statistics will appear in the next Records Committee publication, was the discoverer of Hal Chase's one major league pitching appearance.

The corrections to the game records pertaining to first-inning runs, most batters hit-by-pitch, most assists, and most intentional walks were discovered and corrected by the vice-chairman of the Records Committee, **Joe Dittmar**. For sending him photocopies of local newspapers, or verifying data, Joe wants to thank **Dan Bennett, Bill Deane, Jim Moore, John O'Malley, Bob Richardson, Rich Topp, Walt Wilson**, and the people at the Cincinnati Public Library. I would also like to thank Joe for his enthusiasm, support, and advice throughout this project.

Jim Smith submitted the entries on most games won in a season by visiting clubs, fewest shutouts in a season in each league, and the corrections to the triple play records.

Frank Williams (Barry McCormick), and **Jim Troisi** (Frank Bowerman) found home runs that were lost to the pre-1920 rules.

The discovery of errors in, and corrections to the records of the five catchers was accomplished by **Bill Deane**.

Herman Krabbenhoft submitted the corrections to the home run performances of Charlie Maxwell and Luke Stuart. Herman credits **Bob Rosiek** with the Maxwell discovery, and **Charlie Bevis** for uncovering Stuart's home run.

The entry on 10-run innings by the Boston Red Sox was another submission from **Frank Williams**.

The 1917 game in which Walter Johnson was given the statistics of Dutch Leonard was discovered by **Neil Munro**. Neil, with help from **Pete Palmer**, is responsible for all the passed ball compilations that appear. They are, I believe, the most comprehensive list of passed ball data ever published.

A special thank you to **Bob McConnell** and **Dave Vincent**, keepers of the McConnell/Tattersall Home Run Log, **Pete Palmer**, and **Bill Deane** for their timely and generous responses to all requests.

Lyle Spatz, Chairman
SABR Records Committee
Olney, Maryland
December 1992

Sources

The following publications were used in researching the data presented here.

Encyclopedias

The Baseball Encyclopedia (Macmillan, eighth edition)

Total Baseball (second edition)

The Sports Encyclopedia: BASEBALL (12th edition)

Guides

The Sporting News: The Complete Baseball Record Book (1992 ed.)

The Spalding Official Base Ball Record

The Reach Official American League Guide

Newspapers

Baltimore American

Baltimore Sun

Boston Globe

Boston Herald

Boston Journal

Boston Post

Brooklyn Eagle

Brooklyn Standard-Union

Chicago Chronicle

Chicago Daily News

Chicago Inter-Ocean

Chicago Tribune

Cincinnati Commercial Tribune

Cincinnati Times Star

Cincinnati Enquirer

Cleveland Plain Dealer

Cleveland Press

Detroit Free Press

Detroit News

New York American

New York Daily News

New York Herald

New York Post

New York Sun

New York Times

New York Tribune

New York World

Philadelphia Bulletin

Philadelphia Inquirer

Philadelphia Press

Pittsburgh Post

Pittsburgh Press

St. Louis Globe-Democrat

St. Louis Post-Dispatch

St. Louis Republic

Washington Evening Star

Washington Herald

Washington Post

The Sporting Life

The Sporting News

Other Sources

Tattersall/McConnell Home Run Log

ICI Sheets, National League, 1891-1902

ICI Sheets, American League, 1901-1904

ICI Sheets, American Association, 1882-1891

ICI Sheets, Union Association, 1884

ICI Sheets, PlayersLeague, 1890

ICI Sheets, Federal League, 1914-1915

Official National League Sheets, 1903-1992

Official American League Sheets, 1905-1992

Dick Rudolph

There is an error on the Boston Braves' official pitching sheets for August 8, 1914. For that date pitchers Dick Rudolph and Paul Strand were each awarded a win for Boston's 10-inning, 4-3 victory over Cincinnati. Later on that season, in the second game of a doubleheader at Brooklyn on October 5th, there is another error. Neither of the two Boston pitchers in that game, Tom Hughes nor Otto Hess, was given credit on the official sheets for the Braves 9-5 win. The win should have been credited to Hughes. These two errors, however, created a false balance (one game with two wins awarded, and one game with no win awarded) and so total wins by Boston pitchers were in balance with the teams total wins. As a result the errors were not immediately apparent.

Here are the facts on the August 8 game.

August 8, 1914, at Boston
Boston 4   Cincinnati 3 (10 Innings)

Cincinnati	1 2 0 0 0 0 0 0 0 = 3
Boston	0 0 0 0 0 0 0 0 3 1 = 4

Dick Rudolph started, pitched eight innings; batted for in eighth.

Paul Strand pitched ninth and 10th innings, finished game.

Rudolph left the game behind 3-0, and so can not be the winning pitcher. In the August 9 edition of the *Boston Globe*, the writer covering the game said," Dick Rudolph pitched great ball and a pleasing feature of the game is that he will not have to stand for defeat..."

The weekly won-lost listings in the *New York Times* and the *Washington Post* credited the win to Strand.

On August 20, when Rudolph defeated Pittsburgh, 6-3 the *Globe* noted that it was his 11th consecutive victory.

In his next appearance, August 24, Rudolph was beaten by Chicago, 9-5. Writing in the *Globe* the next day, J.C. O'Leary said, "Rudolph's string of successive wins was interrupted just one shy of an even dozen".

Under "Individual Feats" on page 17 of *The Reach Official American League Guide* covering the 1914 season it says,"Pitcher Rudolph won 11 straight games in August."

Here are the facts on the Hughes-Hess game.

October 5, 1914 at Brooklyn
Boston 9 Brooklyn 5 (second game)

Boston	0 0 3 0 0 0 1 0 5 = 9
Brooklyn	0 0 0 1 0 0 0 4 0 = 5

Tom Hughes started, pitched 8 innings; batted for in 9th.

Otto Hess pitched ninth inning, finished game.

Hughes left the game with the lead, and should be credited with the win.

The weekly won-lost listings in the *New York Times* and the *Washington Post* credited the win to Hughes.

Effects

Tom Hughes

1914 Won-Lost	2-0
1914 Won-Lost Percentage	1.000
Lifetime Won-Lost	56-39
Lifetime Won-Lost Percentage	.589

Dick Rudolph

1914 Won-Lost	26-10
1914 Won-Lost Percentage	.722
1914 consecutive game winning streak	11
Lifetime Won-Lost	121-108
Lifetime Won-Lost Percentage	.528

Paul Strand's 1914 record stays at 6-2.

Otto Hess' 1914 record stays at 5-6.

Rudolph had been credited with having the franchise record for consecutive games won, with 12. However, even if he had in fact won 12 straight, not the 11 that he actually had, it would still not have been a team record. Charlie Buffinton, in 1884, Fred Klobedanz, in 1897, and Ted Lewis in 1898, all had consecutive winning streaks of 13 games for the Boston National League club. Tom Glavine, pitching for Atlanta, tied the franchise record with 13 consecutive wins in 1992.

Cy Young

There are some discrepancies in the won-lost record compiled by Cy Young in his rookie year,

1890. While all sources agree that he had nine wins, in some record books he is charged with only six losses. Young actually had seven losses in his rookie year. In 1890 Young was a member of the National League Cleveland Spiders. The following table documents each of Young's appearances in 1890.

All of Young's appearances were complete games, with one exception, a relief appearance at Brooklyn on August 29. It is his loss in this game that has been missed by several record books and encyclopedias.

August 29, 1890, at Brooklyn
Brooklyn 10   Cleveland 6

| Cleveland | 2 0 2 2 0 0 0 0 = 6 |
| Brooklyn | 4 1 0 0 5 0 0 0 X = 10 |

Ed Beatin started for Cleveland, pitched one inning.

Cy Young pitched final seven innings.

When Young took over in the second inning Cleveland trailed, 4-2. However, they came back to

Date	Opponent	Score	IP	Hits	Runs	BB	K	W/L	Record
Aug. 6	CHI (H)	8-1	9	3	1	3	5	W	1-0
Aug. 9	CIN (H)	5-4	10	9	4	0	3	W	2-0
Aug. 13	PIT (H)	20-9	9	12	9	1	1	W	3-0
Aug. 16	CIN (A)	0-10	8	17	10	0	0	L	3-1
Aug. 22	BOS (A)	8-6	9	7	6	3	1	W	4-1
Aug. 27	PHI (A)	2-4	8	8	4	1	2	L	4-2
Aug. 29	BKL (A)	6-10	7	7	6	1	1	L	4-3
Sep. 1	NY (A)	0-4	9	12	4	4	2	L	4-4
Sep. 11	CHI (A)	0-5	9	6	5	3	2	L	4-5
Sep. 12	HI (A)	4-11	8	14	11	1	1	L	4-6
Sep. 15	PIT (H)	8-3	9	8	3	1	3	W	5-6
Sep. 18	PIT (A)*	11-10	9	8	10	2	4	W	6-6
Sep. 22	BOS (H)	5-4	8	8	4	3	6	W	7-6
Sep. 25	NY (H)	3-4	10.2	12	4	1	2	L	7-7
Oct. 2	PHI (H)	2-2	9	3	2	3	3	T	7-7
Oct. 4	Phi (H) (1G)	5-1	9	5	1	1	1	W	8-7
Oct. 4	Phi (H) (2G)	7-3	7	7	3	0	1	W	9-7
1890 Totals			147.2	146	87	28	38		9-7

* game played at Canton, OH

take a 6-5 lead after four innings, but Brooklyn scored five runs off Young in the last of the fifth to go ahead, 10-6. That was the final score, so this is clearly Young's loss.

Effects

Cy Young

1890 Won-Lost	9-7
1890 Won-Lost Percentage	.563
Lifetime Won-Lost	511-316
Lifetime Won-Lost Percentage	.618

Ed Beatin

1890 Won-Lost	22-30
1890 Won-Lost Percentage	423
Lifetime Won-Lost	48-56
Lifetime Won-Lost Percentage	.462

Hugh Duffy

The corrections to Hugh Duffy's record are for errors on his ICI sheets for the years 1891, 1894, and 1896.

1891

In 1891, Duffy was a member of the American Association Boston Reds.

June 30, 1891, at Boston
Boston 16   Washington 4

The ICI sheets for the day credit Duffy with a single, a home run, and five RBI, when in fact he had no singles, two home runs, and six RBI. He hit a grand slam in the second inning, and a two run homer in the fifth. Both home runs were hit against Kid Carsey.

In the second, Cub Stricker was at third, Paul Radford at second, and Bill Joyce at first, when Duffy drove one over the left field wall. In the fifth inning he again hit one over the left field wall, this time with Tom Brown on first base.

July 4, 1891, at Boston
Boston 10   Columbus 3 (second game)

The ICI sheets fail to give Duffy an RBI for this game, when he should be credited with one. In the ninth inning, after Jack Easton had retired Radford, Tom Brown singled and stole second. Duffy followed with a single to left field scoring Brown.

Effects

Hugh Duffy, 1891

Singles	143
Home Runs	9
Runs Batted In	110
Total Bases	243
Slugging Average	.453

Duffy's 110 RBI ties him with teammate Duke Farrell for most in the American Association for 1891.

1894

In 1894 Duffy was a member of the National League Boston Beaneaters.

June 1, 1894, at Boston
Cleveland 22   Boston 8

In this game Duffy had a home run and three RBI, not, as the ICI sheets show, a single and two RBI. The home run, off Cleveland pitcher Cy Young, came in the fifth inning.

June 20, 1894, at Boston
Boston 13   Baltimore 12

Trailing 12-10, Boston scored three runs in the last of the ninth to top Baltimore, 13-12. Frank Connaughton led off the inning by drawing a walk. A double by Bobby Lowe brought him home to make the score, 12-11. Then with Lowe on third, Herman Long on second, and one man out, Duffy hit a pitch from Sadie McMahon over the left field wall. Under the rules of the time, Duffy should be credited with a triple and two runs driven in, not as the ICI shows with a home run and three RBI. He also should have one fewer run scored.

The following is the explanation given by *The Baseball Encyclopedia* (Macmillan) of the rule in effect prior to 1920.

"When the team batting last won the game in the ninth or an extra inning, the ruling was that the team could not win by more than one run. If a man hit an outside-the-park home run, which under present rules, would have resulted in a victory of more than one run, he was given credit for the lesser hit and only the winning run counted."

Duffy's name should be added to that list of players who lost home runs because of this rule.

Effects

Hugh Duffy, 1894

Singles	152
Triples	16
Runs	160
Total Bases	374
Slugging Average	.694

1896

In 1896, Duffy was a member of the National League Boston Beaneaters.

June 12, 1896 at Boston
Boston 15   Cincinnati 3

ICI sheets for this game give Duffy a home run and one RBI. Because the home run, with two out in the second inning off Red Ehret, came with Bobby Lowe on base, he should be given two RBI.

Effects

Hugh Duffy, 1896

Runs Batted In	113

Hugh Duffy, Lifetime

Singles	1,732
Triples	119
Home Runs	106
Runs Batted In	1,302
Runs	1,552
Total Bases	3,163
Slugging Average	.449

Tris Speaker

The corrections to Tris Speaker's record are for the years 1908, 1911, 1913, 1914, 1926, and 1928. In the years, 1908, 1911, 1913, and 1914 Speaker was a member of the Boston Red Sox. In 1926, he was a member of the Cleveland Indians, and in 1928 he was a member of the Philadelphia Athletics.

1908

September 10, 1908, at Washington
Boston 7   Washington 1

In this game the official fielding performances of Speaker and Boston left fielder, Denny Sullivan were reversed on the American League official sheets.

Speaker should be credited with one assist and three putouts; Sullivan with no assists and two putouts. It may be that Speaker's and Sullivan's batting statistics were also reversed on their official sheets. Evidence for this is inconclusive, but the investigation continues.

Effects

Denny Sullivan, 1908

Assists	17
Putouts	194
Fielding Average	.982 (unchanged)

Denny Sullivan, Lifetime

Assists	33
Putouts	493
Fielding Average	.987

Tris Speaker, 1908

Assists	9
Putouts	58
Fielding Average	1.000 (unchanged)

1911

The error in this year is one of addition. In summing Speaker's official American league day-by-day sheets, his at-bats add to 500. They were incorrectly shown as adding to 510.

Effects

Tris Speaker, 1911

At Bats	500
Batting Average	.334
Slugging Average	.502

1913

The error in this year is one, unfortunately, that is common. For some reason, the *Baseball Guides* that cover the year 1913, do not agree, for many players, with the official league sheets. In this case, the official sheets, which are verifiable by way of the day-by-day sheets, are the more accurate source. On Speaker's official American league day-by-day sheets, his hits add to 189. They have at times been incorrectly shown as 190.

Effects

Tris Speaker, 1913

Hits	189
Singles	129
Total Bases	277
Batting Average	.363
Slugging Average	.533

1914

There is an error on the official American League sheets for the second game of a doubleheader played between Boston and St. Louis on July 22, 1914.

July 22, 1914, at Boston
Boston 6   St. Louis 2 (second game)

Although the Red Sox defeated the Browns in this game by a score of 6-2, the official sheets show the final score as 5-2. Under the runs scored column they omitted a run scored by Speaker.

The score was tied, 1-1 when Boston batted in the bottom of the third inning. With two out, Speaker drew a walk. Duffy Lewis followed with a line-drive to left field. When the ball was misplayed by leftfielder Burt Shotton, it allowed Speaker to come all the way around to score.

The six Boston runs were scored by six different players: Harry Hooper, Tris Speaker, Duffy Lewis, Larry Gardner, Hal Janvrin, and Dick Hoblitzell.

Effects

Tris Speaker, 1914

Runs	101

1926

The error this year is also one of addition. In summing Speaker's official American League day-by-day sheets, his at-bats add to 539. They were incorrectly shown as adding to 540.

Effects

Tris Speaker, 1926

At Bats	539
Batting Average	.304 (unchanged)
Slugging Average	.469 (unchanged)

1928

Once again, the error is one of addition. Speaker's official day-by-day American League sheets were incorrectly shown as adding to 23 instead of 22. The error occurred on July 17 in the second game of a doubleheader at Philadelphia. In this game, won by Detroit, 11-6, Speaker hit one double, which was correctly entered. However his cumulative total went from 21 to 23, instead of to 22. It was the last double of the year for Speaker, and the last of his career.

Effects

Tris Speaker, 1928

Doubles	22
Total Bases	86
Slugging Average	.450

Tris Speaker, Lifetime

At Bats	10,197
Runs	1,882
Stolen Bases	433
Hits	3,514
Singles	2,382
Doubles	792
Triples	223
Total Bases	5,103
Batting Average	.345
Slugging Average	.500 (unchanged)
Assists	449
Putouts	6,787
Fielding Average	.970 (unchanged)

Herman Long

The corrections to Herman Long's record are for errors on his ICI sheets for the years 1891, 1892, and 1894. In each of those years, Long played for the National League Boston Beaneaters.

1891

April 22, 1891, at New York
Boston 4   New York 3

This was opening day of the 1891 season. Although the game was played in New York, the Giants chose to bat first. Facing Amos Rusie, Long led off the bottom of the first by hitting a ball into the the overflow crowd, and making his way around the bases to score. There is some controversy regarding the scoring of this hit, but numerous newspaper accounts refer to a triple and a wild throw to the plate by Rusie. This has been confirmed by the Tattersall/McConnell Home Run Log. Therefore Long is credited with a triple and no RBI for this game.

August 27, 1891, at Cleveland
Boston 12   Cleveland 2 (8 innings)

ICI credited Long with a double, a triple and four RBI. He actually had a double, a home run and five RBI. In the second inning, he hit a fly ball to center fielder George Davis that scored King Kelly from third base for his first RBI of the game. In the sixth inning, with John Clarkson on third, he doubled for his second RBI. Finally, in the eighth inning, facing Ed Beatin, he hit a three-run homer, scoring Kelly and Clarkson ahead of him.

September 19, 1891 at Boston
Boston 11   Pittsburgh 3 (1st game)

In the fifth inning of this game, Long hit a home run off Silver King, with Joe Quinn aboard. ICI correctly shows Long with two RBI but gives him a single instead of a home run.

Effects

Herman Long, 1891

Singles	121
Triples	12
Home Runs	9
Runs Batted In	75
Total Bases	235
Slugging Average	.407

1892

June 14, 1892, at Boston
Boston 11   Cincinnati 6

For this game, ICI correctly gives Long a home run, but incorrectly gives him only one RBI. The home run came in the fourth inning off Jesse Duryea with Hugh Duffy on base.

Effects

Herman Long, 1892

Runs Batted In	78

1894

June 7, 1894, at Boston
Boston 18   St. Louis 7

Long scored three runs in this game, one each in the first, sixth, and seventh innings. On the ICI sheets this game is shown as a 19-7 Boston victory, with Long erroneously given a fourth run scored. If you subtract from the Boston team total this run, and the one given to Hugh Duffy for his June 20 outside-the-park home run, then Bostons total runs scored for 1894 should be 1,220. This, however, remains the all-time major league record for most runs scored by a team in a single season.

Effects

Herman Long, 1894

Runs	136

Herman Long, Lifetime

Singles	1,597
Triples	97
Home Runs	91
Runs	1,456
Runs Batted In	1,054
Total Bases	2,936
Slugging Average	.383

Lou Gehrig

This entry deals with Lou Gehrig's 1926 RBI total, and with some related errors in the records for other Yankees that year.

There are three incorrect entries on Gehrig's official day-by-day sheets. They are for the games of June 25 (2nd game), September 19, and September 26 (2nd game).

June 25, 1926 at Boston
New York 11 Boston 4 (second game)

The official sheets give Gehrig one RBI. He should be credited with two. In the sixth inning Collins and Combs singled. Both scored on Gehrig's triple.

September 19, 1926 at Cleveland
New York 8 Cleveland 3

The official sheets give Gehrig one RBI. He should be credited with four. In the first inning, with two men out, he doubled off Dutch Levsen, scoring Earle Combs who had singled. In the third inning he again doubled with two out off Levsen, this time scoring Babe Ruth who had walked. In the fifth inning, after the first two batters had been retired, Bob Meusel doubled. Gehrig followed with his third double of the game off Levsen, scoring Meusel. In the seventh inning Gehrig hit a solo home run off Levsen for his fourth RBI of the game.

There are other errors on the Yankee's official sheet for this game.

1. No strikeout is credited to Gehrig. He should have one. In the ninth inning he was struck out by Joe Shaute.
2. No strikeouts are credited to catcher Pat Collins. He should have two. He was struck out twice by Levsen; once in the second inning and again in the sixth inning.

3. Both center fielder Earl Combs and short-stop Mike Gazella are given credit for runs batted in; neither player had one.

September 26, 1926 at St. Louis
St. Louis 6 New York 2 (second game)

The official sheets give one RBI to Gehrig, and one to left fielder Ben Paschal. Gehrig should be credited with two, and Paschal with none. In the first inning, after St. Louis pitcher Ernie Wingard retired the first two batters, he gave up a single to Paschal. Gehrig followed with a home run into the right field seats, scoring Paschal ahead of him.

On Babe Ruth's official sheet for 1926 he is credited with 155 runs batted in. There are, however two addition errors on these sheets. On page one, the daily entry for RBI for April 13 through May 18, adds to a total of 44, not the 54 shown as the sub-total at the bottom of the page. On page two, the daily entry for RBI for May 19 through June 14 adds to a total of 29, not the 28 credited in the sub-total at the bottom of the page. Therefore, from the beginning of the season, April 13, through June 14, Ruth was erroneously credited with 82 runs batted in. His correct total for that period is 73, and his correct total for the 1926 season is 146. There may be other errors on Ruth's early official sheets, and members continue to research his lifetime RBI total.

Effects

Lou Gehrig

1926 Runs Batted In	112
1926 Strikeouts	73
Lifetime Runs Batted In	1,995
Lifetime Strikeouts	790

Earle Combs

1926 Runs Batted In	55
Lifetime Runs Batted In	632

Mike Gazella

1926 Runs Batted In	20
Lifetime Runs Batted In	50

Ben Paschal

1926 Runs Batted In	32
Lifetime Runs Batted In	138

Pat Collins

1926 Strikeouts	56
Lifetime Strikeouts	201

Babe Ruth

1926 Runs Batted In	146

Walter Johnson

The correction to Walter Johnson's official sheets are for the years 1912 and 1917.

1912

In 1912, Walter Johnson became the first American League pitcher to win 16 consecutive games. The streak, which lasted from July 3 to August 23, was well publicized in the daily press and acknowledged by AL president, Ban Johnson.

Yet, one of the games that is credited as being part of the streak, (a 10-inning 8-7 win over Chicago on August 5) is listed in the official American League sheets as a win, not for Johnson, but for his teammate, Carl Cashion.

August 5, 1912, at Chicago
Washington 8 Chicago 7 (10 innings)

Washington	0 0 1 0 0 2 1 3 0 1	= 8
Chicago	1 0 6 0 0 0 0 0 0 0	= 7

Bob Groom started for Washington, pitched 2.1 innings.

Carl Cashion pitched 5.1 innings.

Walter Johnson pitched 2.1 innings, finished game.

In this era, an American League official scorer recommended which pitchers were to be assigned the win and loss for each game. The recommendation was reviewed by league president Ban Johnson who made the final decision.

Walter Johnson, who pitched 2.1 hitless, scoreless innings and drove in the winning run, was clearly Washington's most effective pitcher this day. In addition, it was the common practice then to award the win to a pitcher, who, during his pitching stint drove in the winning run. The weekly listings in both the *Washington Post* and the *New York Times* indicate that Johnson was named by the official scorer as the winning pitcher. And since Ban Johnson put his official stamp of approval on the 16-game winning streak, it is obvious that he agreed with the scorer. Mention of Johnson's winning streak appeared in the 1913 *Reach Official American League Guide*, p.207-208, and in the 1913 *Spalding Official Base Ball Record*, p.57. In both publications the August 5 game is included in the 16-game streak.

It was probably simple clerical error that resulted in the official sheets showing Cashion as the winner. Further evidence that this win rightly belongs to Walter Johnson was provided in 1917 by Al Munro Elias, who published in a Washington newspaper an account of Johnson's lifetime pitching record to that time. It shows his won-lost record for 1912 against each of the other seven teams added to 33 wins, 12 losses. This includes the August 5 win in Chicago, which gave Johnson a season record of 9-1 against the White Sox, equalling the major league record for most wins ever against one club in a single season. In the *Spalding Record Books*, 1919-1922, Johnson's nine wins against Chicago in 1912 is listed under "Noteworthy Performances". The nine wins are also mentioned on page 59 of the 1923 *Little Red Book*.

If Johnson did indeed have a 16-game winning streak—a fact that is agreed upon by all sources both then and now—then we have to recognize that a clerical error was made on the August 5 official sheet, and accept that 33rd win. His winning streak and his season's total wins can not be reconciled in any other way. Therefore Johnson's record for 1912 should read 33-12, not 32-12, and his lifetime win total is not 416, but 417.

Another error, albeit a minor one appears on Johnson's official sheet for September 2, 1912. Pitching at home against Philadelphia, he pitched ten innings in a complete game 9-7 loss to the Athletics. The official sheets credit him with only nine innings pitched.

Effects

Walter Johnson, 1912

Won-Lost	33-12
Won-Lost Percentage	.733
Innings	369

Carl Cashion

1912 Won-Lost	10-6
1912 Won-Lost Percentage	.625
Lifetime Won-Lost	12-13
Lifetime Won-Lost Percentage	.480

1917

September 11, 1917 at Washington
Washington 4   Boston 3

On Johnson's official sheet for this game, he was, for many categories, erroneously given the pitching record of the opposing pitcher, Dutch Leonard. This was not a case of the two records being switched, but rather of both pitchers being credited with Leonard's statistics. Therefore no change to Leonard's record is necessary.

	Incorrect	Correct
Opponent At Bats	36	32
Earned Runs	4	0
Hits	13	2
Walks	1	2
Wild Pitches	1	0

Additionally, there are two games earlier in 1917 in which Johnson pitched eight-inning complete games, but was erroneously credited on his official sheet with nine innings pitched. They were both road games that Washington lost.

June 23, 1917, at Boston
Boston 5   Washington 0 (first game)

In this game, Dutch Leonard shut out Washington, 5-0. Incidentally, the Boston starter in the second game of this doubleheader was Babe Ruth. Ruth was ejected from the game by umpire Brick Owens after arguing about a walk to the first batter. His replacement was Ernie Shore. The baserunner, Ray Morgan, was thrown out stealing, and Shore retired the next 26 batters for a perfect game.

July 19, 1917, at St. Louis
St. Louis 4   Washington 2

Allen Sothoron defeated Washington, 4-2.

Effects

Walter Johnson, 1917

Opponent At Bats	1,173
Innings	326
Earned Runs	80
Earned Run Average	2.21
Hits	248
Walks	68
Wild Pitches	7
Opponents Batting Average	.211

Walter Johnson, Lifetime

Won-Lost	417-279
Won-Lost percentage	.599

Frank Williams, and other members of the Records Committee continue to review Walter Johnson's career on a game-by-game basis. There are early indications that there may be several additional errors on his official sheets. We are showing here only won-lost data for his lifetime record. We hope to have a more detailed list of his lifetime accomplishments in a future publication.

Eddie Collins and Buck Weaver

The Chicago White Sox and St. Louis Browns played a doubleheader at Chicago on September 4, 1920. In the second game, won by the White Sox, 5-2, the batting lines for Eddie Collins, who batted third, and Buck Weaver, who batted second, were reversed on the official day-by-day sheets.

Their actual batting performances for that game were:

	AB	R	H	2B	RBI	SH
Eddie Collins	4	2	2	1	1	0
Buck Weaver	3	0	0	0	0	1

In addition, Collins, by batting safely in this game, should be credited with a 22-game hitting streak, (August 21 through September 13).

Effects

Eddie Collins, 1920

At bats	602
Hits	224
Batting Average	.372
Runs	117
Runs Batted In	76
Doubles	38

Eddie Collins, Lifetime

At bats	9,949
Hits	3,312
Batting Average	.333 (unchanged)
Runs	1,821
Runs Batted In	1,300
Doubles	438

Buck Weaver, 1920

At bats	629
Hits	208
Batting Average	.331
Runs	102
Runs Batted In	74
Doubles	34

Buck Weaver, Lifetime

At bats	4,809
Hits	1,308
Batting Average	.272 (unchanged)
Runs	623
Runs Batted In	420
Doubles	198

Bob Groom

On page 61 of *The Sporting News: The Complete Baseball Record Book* (1992 ed.), there are records listed for "Most Consecutive Games Lost, League" and for "Most Consecutive Games Lost, Season." For the American League, the record-holder in both of these categories is said to be Bob Groom, with 19 consecutive losses for Washington in 1909.

These "records" were tied by John Nabors of Philadelphia in 1916. But actually, Groom lost only 15 consecutive games in 1909, so both records belong solely to Nabors. In the 1923 *Little Red Book*, p.59, Nabors is shown as being the *only* pitcher with a one-season 19 game losing streak.

The error in Groom's record was the result of a mistake on the official sheets for the first game of a doubleheader between Washington and Boston on July 5. Going into that game, Groom had lost his last four decisions, and had a record of 5-11.

July 5, 1909 at Boston
Washington 7   Boston 6 (first game)

Washington	3 0 0 0 2 2 0 0 0	= 7
Boston	0 3 2 0 0 1 0 0 0	= 6

Long Tom Hughes started for Washington, pitched two innings.

Bob Groom relieved with none out in the third inning, pitched seven innings, finished game.

When Groom relieved starter Hughes with nobody out in the third inning, Washington trailed, 5-3. Groom pitched the final seven innings, allowing only one run, while Washington scored two in the fifth and two in the sixth to win the game, 7-6. Clearly, Groom was the winning pitcher in this game, breaking his four-game losing streak.

American League official pitching sheets for July 5 show Groom with an appearance, but with no decision; for Hughes a decision is shown, but inexplicably it is a loss. For Groom, this was his sixth win of the year. He went on to lose his next 15 decisions, before defeating Cleveland, in his last appearance of the year, 7-3.

In those years, pitchers' won-lost records were not reconciled with teams won-lost records, and so this error was not caught. On page 49 of the 1910 Reach Guide, Hughes is credited with a 4-8 record and Groom with a 6-26 record. They should read 4-7 and 7-26 respectively.

Effects

Long Tom Hughes

1909 Won-Lost	4-7
1909 Percentage	.364
Lifetime Won-Lost	131-175
Lifetime Percentage	.428

Bob Groom

1909 Won-Lost	7-26
1909 Percentage	.212
1909 Losing Streak	15
Lifetime Won-Lost	119-150
Lifetime Percentage	.442

Also on page 61 of *The Sporting News: The Complete Baseball Record Book* (1992 ed.), Groom is listed as holding the records for "Most Games Lost, Rookie Season" and for "Most Consecutive Games Lost, Rookie Season."

Groom does indeed hold both of these records, but in both cases there is an error in the description. He does have the longest consecutive game losing streak by an AL rookie, but it was 15, not 19.

Also Groom does hold the AL record for most games lost in a season by a rookie, 26. But his record should read (won 7 lost 26, .212).

Chick Stahl

The correction to Chick Stahl's record is for an error on his ICI sheet for August 30, 1899. Stahl was a member of the National League Boston Beaneaters.

August 30, 1899, at Cleveland
Boston 8   Cleveland 5

ICI sheets show Stahl with a single, a home run and one RBI in this game. The home run should be changed to a triple, and no RBI credited. In the ninth inning, Stahl tripled to deep center. He scored on a wild throw to the plate by shortstop, Harry Lochhead. Box scores of the game show Stahl with two hits (single and triple) and four total bases.

Effects

Chick Stahl, 1899

Triples	19
Home Runs	7
Runs Batted In	52
Total Bases	284
Slugging Average	.493

Chuck Stahl, Lifetime

Triples	118
Home Runs	36
Runs Batted In	622
Total Bases	2109
Slugging Average	.416

Roger Connor

The correction to Roger Connor's record is for an error on his ICI sheet for June 2, 1890. Connor was a member of the Players' League New York Giants.

June 2, 1890, at New York
New York 10   Boston 7

ICI sheets show Connor with a single and a run-batted-in. He should be credited with a home run and one RBI. Leading off the eighth inning, Connor hit an inside-the-park home run against Boston pitcher, Matt Kilroy.

Effects

Roger Connor, 1890

Singles	116
Home Runs	14 (led league)
Total Bases	265
Slugging Average	.548 (led league)

Roger Connor, Lifetime

Singles	1,655
Home Runs	138
Total Bases	3,788
Slugging Average	.486

Hardy Richardson

The corrections to Hardy Richardson's record are for errors on his ICI sheets for 1890, and for 1891. In 1890 Richardson was a member of the Players' League Boston Reds, in 1891 Richardson was a member of the American Association Boston Reds.

1890

April 26, 1890, at Boston
Boston 14 New York 10 (8 innings)

ICI sheets give Richardson two singles, a double and two RBI. He should be credited with a single, a double, a home run and four RBI. In the second inning Richardson singled to score Tom Brown from second base. In the sixth inning, with Ed Crane pitching for New York, Brown led off with a single and Richardson followed with a home run over the left field fence. His fourth RBI came when his seventh-inning hit scored King Kelly.

May 22, 1890, at Boston
Boston 7   Pittsburgh 4

ICI sheets show Richardson with a single, a double and three RBI. It should be a home run a double, and three RBI. In the second inning after Dan Brouthers led off with a walk against Pittsburgh pitcher, Al Maul, Richardson homered over the left field fence. Richardson's third RBI came on a fifth-inning double, that again scored Brouthers.

June 5, 1890, at Philadelphia
Boston 9   Philadelphia 4

Richardson's home run is shown on ICI sheets as a two-run homer, giving him two RBI for the game. The home run, which came in the second inning off Ben Sanders, was hit with Art Irwin and Tom Brown on base, so Richardson should be credited with three RBI.

Effects

Hardy Richardson, 1890

Singles	128
Home Runs	13
Runs Batted In	146
Total Bases	274
Slugging Average	.494

1891

August 18, 1891, at Boston
Boston 13   Baltimore 9

ICI sheets show Richardson with a home run and three RBI. The home run was with the bases loaded, and therefore Richardson should be credited with four RBI for this game. The blow, over the left field fence, came in the second inning off Oriole pitcher, John Healy. The base-runners were Hugh Duffy at third, Duke Farrell at second, and Dan Brouthers (on with an intentional walk) at first.

Effects

Hardy Richardson, 1891

Runs Batted In	52

Hardy Richardson, Lifetime

Singles	1,189
Home Runs	70
Runs Batted In	822
Total Bases	2,453
Slugging Average	.435

Harry Stovey

The correction to Harry Stovey's record is for an error on his ICI sheet for September 20, 1890. Stovey was a member of the Players' League Boston Reds.

September 20, 1890, at Chicago
Boston 5   Chicago 3

The ICI sheets show Stovey with one hit, a triple, and no runs-batted-in. However, Stovey's hit was a home run, and he should be credited with one RBI. The home run came in the third inning, when he drove one of Silver King's pitches over the head of left-fielder Tip O'Neill.

Effects

Harry Stovey, 1890

Triples	11
Home Runs	12
Runs Batted In	84
Total Bases	226
Slugging Average	.470

Harry Stovey, Lifetime

Triples	174
Home Runs	122
Runs Batted In	548 (incomplete)
Total Bases	2830
Slugging Average	.461

Dan Brouthers

The correction to Dan Brouthers' record is for an error on his ICI sheet for July 4, 1891. Brouthers was a member of the American Association Boston Reds.

July 4, 1891, at Boston
Boston 10   Columbus 3 (second game)

Brouthers' home run is shown on the ICI sheets as a two-run home run, giving him two RBI for the game. It was actually a three-run home run, and therefore he should be credited with three RBI. In the ninth inning, Tom Brown singled and stole second. Hugh Duffy followed with a single to left field which scored Brown. Jack McGeachey then walked, so two were on when Brouthers came to the plate. Brouthers drove Jack Easton's first pitch over the right-field wall. It was only the third time a ball had been hit over that wall.

Effects

Dan Brouthers, 1891

Runs Batted In	109

Dan Brouthers, Lifetime

Runs Batted In	1,296

Mike Tiernan

The correction to Mike Tienan's record is for an error on his ICI sheet for October 3, 1891. Tiernan was a member of the National League New York Giants.

October 3, 1891, at New York
New York 7   Brooklyn 3

This was the final game of the 1891 season. The ICI sheets give Tiernan a home run and an RBI. He did have an RBI in this game, but his hit was a single, not a home run.

Effects

Mike Tiernan, 1891

Singles	108
Home Runs	16
Total Bases	268
Slugging Average	.494

Mike Tiernan, Lifetime

Singles	1,310
Home Runs	106
Total Bases	2,732
Slugging Average	.463

Because Tiernan hit 16 home runs in 1891, and not 17, he drops into a tie with Harry Stovey of Boston for the NL home run crown.

Tiernan had been thought to be tied with Stovey for Total Base leadership with 271, but by substituting a single for a home run he loses three total bases to finish second with 268.

The loss of the three total bases also means he was not the league leader in slugging average, with .500, but a second place finisher, with .494. Stovey wins that title, too, with a slugging average of .498.

Bobby Lowe

The correction to Bobby Lowe's record is for an error on his ICI sheet for May 11, 1893. Lowe was a member of the National League Boston Beaneaters.

May 11, 1893, at Brooklyn
Boston 9   Brooklyn 8

For this game the ICI sheets show Lowe with a single and four RBI. Lowe did not have a single in this game. His four RBI came as the result of a grand-slam home run. When Lowe came to bat in the fifth inning, Tommy Tucker was on first base, Tommy McCarthy on second, and Hugh Duffy on third. Lowe drove a pitch from George Haddock into left field, where it got by Brooklyn left-fielder George Shoch for an inside-the-park grand-slam home run.

Effects

Bobby Lowe, 1893

Singles	119
Home Runs	14
Total Bases	228
Slugging Average	.433

Bobby Lowe, Lifetime

Singles	1,543
Home Runs	71
Total Bases	2,542
Slugging Average	.360

Hal Chase

Most record books and encyclopedias seem to have missed Hal Chase's one major-league pitching appearance. It came on July 25, 1908, while he was a member of the New York Yankees.

July 25, 1908, at Detroit
Detroit 5   New York 3

After seven and one-half innings, the Highlanders, behind Jack Chesbro, were leading the Tigers, 3-2. But in the Detroit eighth, after one man had been retired, Germany Schaefer and Sam Crawford hit back-to-back singles. Ty Cobb followed with a triple, scoring both runners, and giving Detroit a 4-3 lead. With left-handed hitter Claude Rossman the next batter, New York manager Kid Elberfeld moved the right-handed Chesbro to first base, and brought first-baseman Chase to the mound. Chase got Rossman out on a fly ball, which scored Cobb, and Elberfeld brought Chesbro back in. Chase's major-league pitching career lasted just one-third of an inning.

Effects

Hal Chase

1908 Innings	.1
1908 Games Pitched	1
Lifetime Innings	.1
Lifetime Games pitched	1

Jack Chesbro, 1908

Complete Games	20
Innings	288.2
Earned Run Average	2.93 (unchanged)
Games at First Base	1

Jack Chesbro, Lifetime

Complete Games	260
Innings	2,896.2
Earned Run Average	2.68 (unchanged)
Games at First Base	1

Most Assists, Game, Nine Innings, Both Clubs

The record book listings in this category are riddled with errors. Of the three highest single-game claims, all are inaccurate according to official league records. Below is a table showing the three present listings with their claimed number of assists versus the number of assists reflected by official league data. Following the errors is a newly-discovered assist record, verified by official data.

In light of this information, we now know that the major league record for assists by both clubs in a nine-inning game is 44 by Cleveland and St. Louis, set on May 27, 1909. The National League record is 43, set by Brooklyn and New York on April 21, 1903.

			Claimed Record		*Official Record*	
League	*Date*	*Teams*	*Total*	*Teams*	*Total*
A.L.	August 21, 1905	New York 23, Chicago 22	45	New York 20, Chicago 21	41
N.L.	April 21, 1903	Brooklyn 23, New York 21	44	Brooklyn 24, New York 19	43
N.L.	May 15, 1909	New York 25, Cincinnati 19	44	New York 25, Cincinnati 17	42
A.L.	May 27, 1909			Cleveland 22, St. Louis 22	44

Game of May 27, 1909

Cleveland	*Assists*	*St. Louis*	*Assists*
Wilbur Good rf	0	Roy Hartzell rf	2
Bill Bradley 3b	1	Art Griggs lf	0
Terry Turner ss	6	Hobe Ferris 3b	2
Nap Lajoie 2b	5	Bobby Wallace ss	4
Bill Hinchman cf	0	Jimmy Williams 2b	2
George Stovall 1b	0	Tom Jones 1b	3
Ted Easterly c	3	John McAleese cf	0
Bris Lord lf	0	Jim Stephens c	3
Addie Joss p	7	Barney Pelty p	6
Total	22	Total	22

Most Runs, Start of Game, With None Out

The major league record for "Most Runs, Start of Game, With None Out" has long been thought to be ten, scored by the New York Giants against the St. Louis Cardinals at the Polo Grounds, May 13, 1911. It is listed as such by *The Sporting News: The Complete Baseball Record Book*, 1992 ed., p.36; and by *The Book of Baseball Records* (Elias), 1991 ed., p.107.

However, according to five newspaper accounts the following day, only seven runs, not ten, scored before the first out was made. Although it is a fact that the first ten Giant batters did indeed score, three of them scored after the 11th batter in the inning, Larry Doyle, had flied out to Rube Ellis. The key at-bat here seems to be that of Josh Devore, the tenth batter of the inning. Devore, the Giants lead-off hitter, was batting for the second time in the first inning. Bob Harmon, who had replaced starter Slim Sallee, was the St. Louis pitcher, Christy Mathewson was the runner at first, and Chief Meyers was the runner at third. All the newspaper accounts agree on what happened next. Devore hit a bouncer back to Harmon, who tried unsuccessfully to catch Meyers off third, leaving all runners safe. Thus, when Doyle batted and made the initial out, the bases were loaded and only seven runs had been scored.

The record rightfully belongs to the Phillies who, in a game at Philadelphia on August 13, 1948, scored nine runs against the Giants before making their first out.

Batter	New York Herald	New York Sun	New York World	New York Tribune	St. Louis Dispatch
Devore	1B, scored; later safe on FC	1B, scored; later safe on FC	1B, scored; later safe on FC	1B, scored; later safe on FC	1B, scored; later safe on FC
Doyle	1B, scored; later flied out to left	1B, scored; later flied out to left	1B, scored; later flied out to left	1B, scored; later flied out to left	1B, scored; later flied out to left
Snodgrass	3B, scored	3B, scored	3B, scored	1B, scored	3B, scored
Murray	BB, scored	BB, scored	BB, scored	BB, scored	BB, scored
Merkle	HR, scored	HR, scored	HR, scored	HR, scored	HR, scored
Bridwell*	safe E-6, scored	?, scored	1B, scored	1B, scored	safe E-1, scored
Devlin	BB, scored	?, scored	BB, scored	BB, scored	BB, scored
Meyers	1B	?	1B	1B	1B
Mathewson	1B	?	1B	1B	1B
Newspaper description	"Doyle made the first out…"	"Doyle, second time up, was the first out…"	"Doyle was the first man in eleven to die."	"Doyle lifted a fly to Ellis for the first out…"	"Doyle flied to Ellis."
*Note	Bridwell safe, E-6	? = not described	Bridwell singled	Snodgrass singled Bridwell singled	Bridwell safe, E-1

Most Intentional Bases on Balls

Since 1955, when intentional walk data began being distinguished from other walks, the most instances in a game is listed as ten, occurring on August 26, 1980, between New York and San Diego. However, recent research has uncovered a game in which 11 intentional bases on balls were issued. On May 2, 1956, the Giants received seven intentional free passes and the Cubs four. New York's seven also ties the one-team record shared by Houston and Chicago (NL).

All of the following data was collected from the official, day-by-day, league records housed in the National Baseball Library, Cooperstown.

Batter	Bases on Balls	
New York	*Total*	*Intent*
Alvin Dark	1	0
Willie Mays	2	2
Dusty Rhodes	1	1
Daryl Spencer	1	0
Don Mueller	1	1
Wes Westrum	3	2
Hank Thompson	1	1
New York Total	**10**	**7**

Batter	Bases on Balls	
New York	*Total*	*Intent*
Al Worthington	3	1
Don Liddle	1	0
Hoyt Wilhelm	2	2
Steve Ridzik	1	0
Marv Grissom	1	0
Windy McCall	0	0
Joe Margoneri	1	1
Ruben Gomez	0	0
New York Total	**9**	**4**

Chicago		
Don Hoak	1	0
Ernie Banks	3	2
Walt Moryn	1	1
Hobie Landrith	1	1
Gale Wade	1	0
Russ Meyer	1	0
Pete Whisenant	1	0
Chicago Total	**9**	**4**
Two-Team Total	**19**	**11**

Chicago		
Russ Meyer	1	1
Turk Lown	1	0
Jim Davis	3	2
Vito Valentinetti	1	0
Jim Brosnan	4	4
Chicago Total	**10**	**7**
Two-Team Total	**19**	**11**

Batters Hit By A Pitch, Both Clubs, Nine-Inning Game

The record for batters hit by a pitch (both clubs) in a nine-inning game since 1900 is seven. Both *The Sporting News: The Complete Baseball Record Book*, 1992 ed., p.49, and *The Book of Baseball Records* (Elias), 1991 ed., p.115 list five games where this occurred, three in the AL and two in the NL.

However, the evidence indicates that in neither of the National League games cited were seven batters hit.

The first game referred to was between New York and Brooklyn, at Brooklyn on July 17,1900. In this game six batters, not seven, were hit. The error seems to have originated from *The Sporting Life's* tally of New York batters hit by Brooklyn's Joe McGinnity. Eight other sources say that only Giants George Davis and Elmer Smith were hit, not the three listed by *The Sporting Life*.

HBP	Brooklyn Eagle	Brooklyn Standard	NY Herald	NY Sun	NY Times	NY Tribune	NY World	Sporting Life	Sporting News
By Doheny (NY)	Sheckard*	1	1	1	1	1	1	1	1
By Mathewson (NY)	Jones* Farrell* Sheckard*	3	3	3	3	3	Jones* Farrell* Sheckard*	3	3
By McGinnity (Brooklyn)	Davis* Smith*	2	2	2	2	2	Davis* Smith*	3	2
Game Total	6	6	6	6	6	6	6	7	6
Balanced Box?	Yes	X	No	X	X	Yes	X	No	Yes

x = no at-bats shown in boxscore; otherwise, box matches *Brooklyn Eagle* and *New York Tribune*.

* = players hit-by-pitch are described in game account

Most Batters Hit By A Pitch, Both Clubs, Nine-Inning Game

The other National League game in error for batters hit by a pitch (both clubs) was the second game of a doubleheader, New York at Boston, on August 1, 1903. Again it is obviously *The Sporting Life* account that is the source of the error. It shows seven batters being hit, while all other accounts show only two.

HBP	Brooklyn Eagle	Brooklyn Standard	NY Herald	NY Sun	NY Times	NY Tribune	NY World	Sporting Life	Sporting News
1st Game Giants HBP	McGann (2) McGraw Gilbert	McGann (2) McGraw Gilbert	4	4	McGann (2) McGraw Gilbert	McGann (2) McGraw Gilbert	4	4	3
!st Game Boston HBP	0	0	0	0	0	0	0	0	0
2nd Game Giants HBP	Warner	Warner	1	1	1	Warner	?	4	1
2nd Game Boston HBP	0	Moran	1	1	1	Moran	?	3	1

The error of listing this game as having had seven hit batters has also caused the record books to be wrong on two other related records.

1. "Most Hit by Pitch, Doubleheader" - The record is shown as eight, the Giants having four batters hit in each game. They in fact had only five-hit, four in the first game, and one in the second.
2. "Most Hit by Pitch, Doubleheader, Both Clubs" - The record is shown as 11, Giant players having been hit eight times, and Boston players having been hit three times. As stated above, the Giants had only five hit in the two games, and Boston had only one.

Most Hit By Pitch, Doubleheader

On page 31 of *The Sporting News: The Complete Baseball Record Book*, there is the category "Most Hit By Pitch, Doubleheader." The National League, and major league record holder is claimed to be Frank Chance, with five. It happened, they say, on May 30, 1904.

Chance, playing for Chicago against the Reds in Cincinnati, did set the record that day for being hit the most times in a doubleheader, but it was four times, not five. He was hit three times in the first game by Jack Harper and once in the second game by Win Kellum. While the National League did not keep official records of batters hit-by-pitch in 1904, newspaper accounts of the game are quite specific in describing each of Chance's at-bats in the doubleheader.

It is uncertain if there are any other players who have been hit four times in a doubleheader. So for now let us say that Chance, with four, still holds the record for being hit the most times in a doubleheader.

From the above newspapers plus the *Cincinnati Post*, the *Chicago Tribune*, and the *Chicago Daily News*, each of Chance's plate appearances can be accounted for. They are as follows:

Cincinnati Commercial Tribune	"He [Chance] felt three raps off Harper's speed in the morning game, and Kellum hit him on the arm in the afternoon."
Cincinnati Enquirer	"In the forenoon, he [Chance] was given a base three times because he was hit… In the afternoon game, Kellum hit Chance fairly in the short ribs, and on another occasion, narrowly missed him."
Cincinnati Times Star	"Chance was hit four times by the pitchers on Monday - three in the morning, once in the afternoon."
Chicago Chronicle	"Chance is pretty badly banged up, the injury on his head being the most severe. He was hit twice on the left arm and once on the body, and in a day or two he is liable to find himself stiff and sore."

Morning Game		*Afternoon Game*	
1st Inning	Hit by a pitch, left on base	1st Inning	Hit by a pitch, scored
4th Inning	Popped out to Kelley (1b)	3rd Inning	Singled, caught stealing
7th Inning	Hit by a pitch, forced at second	6th Inning	Fouled out to Donlin (lf)
9th Inning	Hit by a pitch, scored	8th Inning	Walked, left on base
		9th Inning	Flied out to end the game

Most Games Won By Visiting Clubs

On page 110 of *The Sporting News: The Complete Baseball Record Book,* 1992 ed., is the following record: "Most Games Won by Visiting Clubs, Season N.L.- (8-club league)—307 in 1948 (lost 308)." The 8-club National League record for most games won by a visiting club in one season is *308.* It has been accomplished twice, in 1917 (304 losses), and again in 1923 (307 losses).

Road Records of National League Teams, 1917

	BOS	BKL	CHI	CIN	NY	PHI	PIT	STL	TOTAL
Boston	—	6-7	7-4	7-4	4-7	3-6	8-3	2-8	37-39
Brooklyn	2-7	—	3-8	7-4	6-7	5-5	8-4	3-8	34-43
Chicago	7-4	7-4	—	4-7	3-8	4-7	8-3	6-5	39-38
Cincinnati	8-3	8-3	7-4	—	5-6	2-9	4-7	5-6	39-38
New York	8-3	6-3	7-4	5-6	—	6-6	9-2	7-4	48-28
Philadelphia	5-8	6-4	9-2	5-6	2-8	—	6-5	8-3	41-36
Pittsburgh	5-6	2-8	2-9	3-8	4-7	3-8	—	7-4	26-50
St. Louis	7-4	3-7	7-4	7-4	4-7	6-5	10-1	—	44-32

308-304

Road Records of National League Teams, 1923

	BOS	BKL	CHI	CIN	NY	PHI	PIT	STL	TOTAL
Boston	—	5-6	3-8	3-8	4-7	8-3	3-8	6-5	32-45
Brooklyn	8-3	—	6-5	3-8	5-6	7-4	5-6	5-6	39-38
Chicago	8-3	7-4	—	5-6	4-7	6-5	3-8	4-7	37-40
Cincinnati	7-4	6-5	7-4	—	7-4	10-0	3-8	5-6	45-31
New York	9-2	5-6	5-6	6-5	—	10-1	7-4	6-4	48-28
Philadelphia	6-5	6-5	4-7	3-9	2-9	—	5-6	4-8	30-49
Pittsburgh	9-2	5-6	3-8	6-5	5-6	7-4	—	5-6	40-37
St. Louis	8-3	6-5	3-8	6-5	3-8	7-3	4-7	—	37-39

308-307

Fewest Shutouts

On page 73 of *The Sporting News: The Complete Baseball Record Book*, 1992 ed., carries the following incorrect entry: "Fewest Shutouts, Season N.L.- (8-club league)— 48 in 1925." The 8-club National League record for fewest shutouts in a season was set in 1925, however the number of shutouts was *49*.

1.	April 14	Pete Donohue	CIN vs STL	4-0	
2.	April 17	Wayland Dean	NY at BOS	2-0	
3.	April 19	Leo Dickerman	STL at CHI	6-0	
4.	April 26	Rube Marquard (8), Bill Ryan (1)	BOS at BKL	3-0	
5.	May 6	Dazzy Vance	BKL at BOS	10-0	
6.	May 9	Flint Rhem	STL at NY	8-0	
7.	May 12	Johnny Cooney	BOS vs CHI	2-0	(1st game)
8.	May 13	Art Nehf	NY vs CIN	3-0	
9.	May 22	Percy Jones	CHI at BKL	2-0	
10.	May 31	Jack Scott	NY at BKL	2-0	
11.	June 5	Dolf Luque	CIN vs BOS	1-0	(10 innings)
12.	June 12	Eppa Rixey	CIN vs BKL	6-0	
13.	June 13	Elmer Jacobs	CHI vs BOS	2-0	
14.	June 17	Dolf Luque	CIN vs NY	1-0	
15.	June 19	Leo Dickerman	STL vs BOS	3-0	
16.	June 27	Art Reinhart	STL vs CHI	5-0	
17.	June 30	Tony Kaufman	CHI vs PIT	1-0	
18.	July 3	Pete Donohue	CIN at PIT	8-0	
19.	July 6	Virgil Barnes	NY vs PHI	6-0	(1st game)
20.	July 7	Pete Donohue	CIN at PHI	4-0	(1st game)
21.	July 10	Larry Benton	BOS vs CIN	1-0	
22.	July 16	Clarence Mitchell	PHI vs CHI	3-0	
23.	July 17	Rube Benton	CIN at BKL	4-0	

24.	July 18	Dolf Luque	CIN at NY	3-0	
25.	July 19	Bill Sherdel	STL at BKL	2-0	
26.	July 26	Dazzy Vance	BKL vs NY	3-0	
27.	July 27	Jakie May	CIN vs STL	3-0	(2nd game)
28.	July 28	Dolf Luque	CIN vs PHI	3-0	
29.	August 8	Johnny Couch	PHI at CHI	2-0	
30.	August 16	Johnny Cooney	BOS at NY	6-0	(1st game)
31.	August 22	Hal Carlson	PHI vs STL	5-0	(2nd game)
32.	August 23	Dazzy Vance	BKL vs CHI	6-0	(1st game)
33.	August 26	Lee Meadows	PIT at BOS	2-0	
34.	August 27	Hal Carlson	PHI vs CHI	4-0	
35.	August 27	Vic Aldridge	PIT at BOS	1-0	
36.	August 30	Allan Sothoron	STL at NY	8-0	(2nd game)
37.	September 1	Larry Benton	BOS vs CHI	2-0	
38.	September 3	Eppa Rixey	CIN at CHI	4-0	(2nd game)
39.	September 5	Tony Kaufman	CHI vs CIN	6-0	(1st game)
40.	September 8	Dazzy Vance	BKL vs PHI	1-0	(1st game)
41.	September 10	Hal Carlson	PHI at BOS	4-0	(1st game)
42.	September 12	Johnny Ring	PHI at BOS	6-0	
43.	September 12	Bill Sherdel	STL vs PIT	4-0	
44.	September 16	Pete Alexander	CHI vs BOS	3-0	(1st game)
45.	September 20	Hal Carlson	PHI at CIN	3-0	
46.	September 23	Allan Sothoron	STL vs NY	8-0	(1st game)
47.	September 24	Jack Scott	NY at PIT	4-0	
48.	September 26	Fred Fitzsimmons	NY at PIT	3-0	(2nd game)
49.	October 3	Dutch Ulrich	PHI vs NY	3-0	(2nd game)

There is disagreement in the various encyclopedias about the record for fewest shutouts in one season in the American League (8-club league). The correct number is *41*, set in 1930.

1.	April 19	Rube Walberg	PHI vs WAS	9-0	
2.	April 20	Willis Hudlin	CLE at DET	2-0	
3.	April 26	General Crowder	STL vs CHI	12-0	
4.	April 30	George Pipgras	NY at WAS	9-0	
5.	May 10	Milt Gaston	BOS vs STL	2-0	
6.	May 12	George Pipgras	NY vs DET	7-0	
7.	May 16	Ad Liska	WAS at PHI	4-0	(2nd game)
8.	May 18	George Pipgras	NY at BOS	11-0	
9.	May 18	Lefty Grove	PHI at WAS	1-0	
10.	May 25	Firpo Marberry	WAS vs BOS	5-0	
11.	June 7	George Uhle	DET vs STL	6-0	
12.	June 8	Waite Hoyt	DET vs STL	1-0	(6 innings)
13.	June 12	Clint Brown	CLE vs PHI	4-0	
14.	June 13	Rip Collins	STL vs BOS	1-0	(11 innings)
15.	June 20	George Earnshaw	PHI vs CLE	8-0	
16.	June 21	Herb Pennock	NY vs DET	3-0	
17.	June 23	Danny MacFayden	BOS vs DET	2-0	
18.	June 23	Hank Johnson	NY vs STL	15-0	
19.	June 24	Bump Hadley	WAS vs CLE	7-0	(5 innings)
20.	July 4	Sam Jones	WAS vs NY	8-0	(1st game)
21.	July 6	Clint Brown	CLE vs STL	7-0	
22.	July 8	Rube Walberg	PHI at NY	4-0	(1st game)
23.	July 15	Firpo Marberry	WAS at DET	3-0	
24.	July 31	Ted Lyons	CHI vs STL	1-0	(2nd game)
25.	August 6	Dick Coffman	STL at CHI	5-0	(1st game)
26.	August 9	Vic Sorrell	DET at BOS	3-0	
27.	August 9	George Earnshaw	PHI vs CHI	3-0	
28.	August 12	Bill Shores	PHI vs CLE	7-0	

29.	August 14	Ed Durham	BOS vs STL	3-0	
30.	August 14	Wes Ferrell	CLE at PHI	15-0	
31.	August 17	Clint Brown	CLE at BOS	2-0	(7 innings)
32.	August 19	Red Ruffing	NY vs CHI	3-0	
33.	August 19	George Blaeholder	STL at PHI	7-0	
34.	August 23	George Earnshaw	PHI vs DET	2-0	
35.	August 23	Lloyd Brown	WAS vs STL	2-0	
36.	August 24	Milt Gaston	BOS vs CHI	2-0	(2nd game)
37.	August 27	Lefty Stewart	STL vs DET	5-0	
38.	August 29	Pat Caraway	CHI at CLE	3-0	(13 innings)
39.	August 30	Lefty Grove	PHI at BOS	11-0	
40.	September 1	Red Ruffing	NY vs PHI	2-0	(2nd game)
41.	September 10	Vic Sorrell	DET vs PHI	4-0	

Lost Home Runs

In addition to Hugh Duffy, we know of two more players—Barry McCormick and Frank Bowerman—who should be added to the list of those who lost home runs because of the rule governing game-winning outside-the-park hits in effect prior to 1920. (see the entry on Hugh Duffy, June 20,1894)

McCormick's misfortune came in the first game of a doubleheader at Washington on August 31, 1903. Going into the last half of the tenth inning the score between Boston and Washington was tied at 1-1. The opposing pitchers were Bill Dinneen for Boston, and Case Patten for Washington.

In the last of the tenth with one out and Bill Clarke aboard, McCormick hit a Dinneen pitch over the left field fence to give the Senators a 2-1 victory. He was credited with a triple.

The other occurrence of a lost home run came on April 30, 1908. As they came to bat in the last of the ninth inning, the home-standing Boston Braves and the New York Giants were in a 2-2 tie. But with Bill Sweeney on second base, Frank Bowerman of Boston hit one into the stands off Doc Crandall of the Giants to defeat New York, 3-2. Because Sweeney's run was the winning run, Bowerman was credited with only a double.

This would bring the list to 40, and it is likely that there are others yet undiscovered.

Games Caught

Errors have been discovered on the official records of the following five catchers: Johnny Bench, Greg Goossen, Bill Plummer, Ted Simmons, and Rube Walker. In each case the errors pertain to the number of games caught in a particular season.

Johnny Bench

Bench is listed as the catcher for Cincinnati in the second game of a doubleheader at home vs Los Angeles on June 21, 1970. In fact, the Reds catcher in this game was Pat Corrales. Bench played right field. The records for Corrales are correct. But Bench's four putouts should be credited to him as an outfielder, as should the home run that he hit in this game.

In San Diego on May 21, 1972, Bench was again mistakenly listed on the official sheets as a catcher. Once again it was in the second game of a doubleheader, but this time the catcher for Cincinnati was Bill Plummer, while Bench played first base. The records for Plummer are correct, but Bench's seven putouts should be credited to him as a first baseman.

Effects

Johnny Bench, 1970

Games Caught	139
Catcher Putouts	755
Fielding Average, Catcher .986 (unchanged)	
Outfield	.926
Games in Outfield	24
Outfield Putouts	24

Johnny Bench, 1972

Games Caught	129
Catcher Putouts	735
Fielding Average, Catcher	.992
First Base	.960
Games at First Base	7
First Base Putouts	24

Johnny Bench, Lifetime

Games Caught	1,742
Catcher Putouts	9,249
Fielding Average, Catcher .990 (unchanged)	
Games in Outfield	111
Outfield Putouts	147
Fielding Average, Outfield	.949
Games at First Base	145
First Base Putouts	966
Fielding Average, First Base	.985

Greg Goossen

Goossen is listed as the catcher for the New York Mets in the second game of a doubleheader at home vs Atlanta on May 19, 1968. However, the Mets catcher in this game was Jerry Grote. Goossen played first base. The records for Grote are correct, but Goossen's one assist and 13 putouts should be credited to him as a first baseman.

Effects

Greg Goossen, 1968

Games Caught	1
Catcher Putouts	7
Catcher Assists	1
Fielding Average, Catcher	.889
First Base .992 (unchanged)	
Games at First Base	31
First Base Putouts	230
First Base Assists	23

Greg Goossen, Lifetime

Games Caught	43
Catcher Putouts	182
Catcher Assists	12
Fielding Average	
Catcher	.975
First Base	.992 (unchanged)
Games at First Base	79
First Base Putouts	604
First Base Assists	54

There are addition errors on the official records of games caught for Rube Walker, while with Brooklyn (1951), Bill Plummer (1972), and Ted Simmons (1977).

Effects

Rube Walker

Games Caught, 1951, Brooklyn	23
Games Caught, 1951, Total	54
Games Caught, Lifetime	466

Bill Plummer

Games Caught, 1972	36
Games Caught, Lifetime	343

Ted Simmons

Games caught, 1977	143
Games caught, Lifetime	1,771

Most Consecutive Home Runs, Two Games

On page 22 of *The Sporting News: The Complete Baseball Record Book*, 1992 ed., there is an entry for "Most Consecutive Home Runs, Two Games." The American League record is 4. The following players are listed from the American League.

Jimmie Foxx, Philadelphia, June 7, June 8, 1933

Hank Greenberg, Detroit, July 26, July 27, 1938

Charlie Maxwell, Detroit, May 3 (1G), May 3 (2G), 1959

Willie Kirkland, Cleveland, July 9 (2nd game), July 13, 1961

*Bobby Murcer, New York, June 24 (1G), June 24 (2G), 1970

Mike Epstein, Oakland, June 15, June 16, 1971

*Don Baylor, Baltimore, July 1, July 2, 1975

Larry Herndon, Detroit, May 16, May 18, 1982

Bo Jackson, Kansas City, July 17, August 26, 1990

(* also base on balls)

The entry for Charlie Maxwell should have an asterisk(*), because there was a base on balls between his second and third home runs. The doubleheader was played against the New York Yankees, at Detroit, on May 3, 1959. Here is the sequence of at-bats involving the home runs.

First Game
In his last at-bat, leading off the seventh inning—home run off Don Larsen.

Second Game

First at bat—1st inning home run off Duke Maas.

Second at bat—walked by Johnny Kucks in second inning.

Third at bat—4th inning home run off Johnny Kucks.

Fourth at bat—7th inning home run off Zack Monroe.

Home Run, First Major League At-Bat

On page 20, of *The Sporting News: The Complete Baseball Record Book*, 1992 ed., there is a list of players who had a "Home Run, First Major League At-Bat." There is a player missing from the American League list—Luke Stuart of the St. Louis Browns. Stuart's home run came on August 8, 1921, making him, rather than Earl Averill (April 16, 1929), the first American Leaguer to homer in his first time at bat.

Stuart made his major league debut on July 28, 1921 against the Yankees. He replaced second baseman Jimmy Austin in the last of the eighth inning, but never came to bat. His next appearance was on August 8, when he replaced Marty McManus at second base in the seventh inning of a game against Washington, at Griffith Stadium. When they came to bat in the ninth inning, the Browns trailed Walter Johnson and the Senators, 16-3. Wally Gerber led off for St. Louis with a single. The next batter, Stuart, in his first major league at-bat followed with a two-run homer off Johnson, making the final score, 16-5.

Triple Plays

On page 100 of *The Sporting News: The Complete Baseball Record Book*, 1992, ed., there is a listing of "Most Triple Plays, Season." It lists records for the different membership sizes for each league.

For the National League as a 12-club league, the record shown is four,—in 1969, 1971, 1978, and 1989. There were, however, three years when, as a 12-club league, the NL had six triple plays—1893, 1894, and 1899.

1893

	Inn	Runners
May 24 Pittsburgh vs St. Louis at Pittsburgh	4	1-2-3
May 26 Brooklyn vs Baltimore at Baltimore	7	1-2-3
June 24 Baltimore vs Boston at Boston	8	1-2
July 20 Baltimore vs Brooklyn at Brooklyn	5	1-2
July 22 Cincinnati vs St. Louis at St. Louis	1	1-2
Sept 8 Washington vs Cleveland at Cleveland	1	1-2-3

1894

	Inn	Runners
May 5 Baltimore vs Washington at Baltimore	8	1-2-3
June 29 St. Louis vs Boston at St. Louis	8	1-2-3
August 14 Chicago vs Brooklyn at Brooklyn	6	1-2
August 15 Boston vs Pittsburgh at Boston	9	1-2

August 18
New York vs Chicago at New York   3   1-2

September 11
Pittsburgh vs Philadelphia at Pittsburgh   8   1-2

1899

	Inn	Runners
Apr. 24 Baltimore vs New York at New York	9	1-2
June 28 St. Louis vs Baltimore at St. Louis	5	1-2-3
July 22 Louisville vs Brooklyn at Louisville	7	1-2
Aug. 14 Cincinnati vs Boston at Boston	1	1-2-3
Aug. 18 Cleveland vs Brooklyn at Brooklyn	2	1-2
Oct. 10 New York vs Brooklyn at Brooklyn	3	1-2

For the National League as a 10-club league, there is no listing. The record is five, accomplished twice, in 1964 and 1965.

1964

	Inn	Runners
May 17 Philadelphia vs Houston at Houston	5	1-2
May 31 New York vs San Francisco at New York	14	1-2
June 4 Milwaukee vs Cincinnati at Milwaukee	2	1-2
Aug. 15 Philadelphia vs New York at New York	2	1-2
Oct. 2 Philadelphia vs Cincinnati at Cincinnati	4	1-2

1965

	Inn	Runners
Apr. 15 New York vs Houston at New York	2	1-3
May 3 San Francisco vs St. Louis at St. Louis	4	1-2
July 14 Chicago vs Milwaukee at Chicago	2	1-3
July 25 Chicago vs Pittsburgh at Chicago	4	1-2
Oct. 3 Chicago vs Pittsburgh at Pittsburgh	5	1-2

For the American League as a 10-club league, there is no listing. The record is five, accomplished in 1968.

1968

	Inn	Runners
June 3 New York vs Minnesota at New York	8	1-2-3
June 23 Washington vs Oakland at Oakland	3	1-2
July 30 Washington vs Cleveland at Cleveland	1	1-2
Sept 1 Detroit vs Baltimore at Detroit	3	1-2
Sept 10 Minnesota vs Cleveland at Minnesota	5	1-2

The major-league record for an eight-club league is seven, for both the National League and the American League. However, there were two additional eight-club major leagues, the American Association and the Players' League, both of whom in 1890 also had seven.

American Association, 1890

	Inn	Runners
Apr. 30 Rochester vs Brooklyn at Rochester	3	1-2-3
May 7 Rochester vs Syracuse at Syracuse	4	2-3
June 15 Rochester vs Syracuse at Syracuse	7	1-2
July 13 St. Louis vs Philadelphia at St. Louis	9	1-2-3
Aug. 21 Philadelphia vs Louisville at Louisville	5	1-2
Sept 14 Baltimore vs Philadelphia at Philadelphia	8	2-3
Oct. 11 Syracuse vs Philadelphia at Philadelphia	1	1-2

Players' League, 1890

	Inn	Runners
June 14 New York vs Brooklyn at Brooklyn	9	1-2
June 30 Boston vs Pittsburgh at Pittsburgh	9	1-2
July 15 Chicago vs Philadelphia at Philadelphia	8	1-2-3
July 30 Chicago vs Brooklyn at Chicago	7	1-2
Aug. 15 Pittsburgh vs Chicago at Chicago	3	1-2
Sept 6 Brooklyn vs New York at Brooklyn	7	1-2
Sept 29 Buffalo vs Boston at Buffalo	9	1-2

Most Innings, League, Scoring 10 Or More Runs

On page 37 of *The Sporting News: The Complete Baseball Record Book*, 1992, ed., there is a listing of "Most Innings, League Scoring 10 or More Runs." The record shown for the American League is 23, by Boston. It should be *24*, by Boston.

1. May 2, 1901, at Philadelphia—

   Boston 23 Philadelphia 12

Boston	2 9 10 0 0 0 0 0 2	= 23
Philadelphia	2 0 2 1 2 0 0 0 5	= 12

2. April 19, 1924, at Boston—

   Boston 12 Philadelphia 0

Philadelphia	0 0 0 0 0 0 0 0 0	= 0
Boston	0 10 0 0 0 1 0 1 X	= 12

3. May 12, 1928, at Boston—

   Boston 15 St. Louis 2

St. Louis	0 0 1 0 0 1 0 0 0	= 2
Boston	0 1 11 1 0 2 0 0 X	= 15

4. July 11, 1929, at Detroit—

   Boston 15 Detroit 8

Boston	1 3 0 0 0 10 0 1 0	= 15
Detroit	0 3 1 0 1 0 1 0 2	= 8

5. August 13, 1933, at Boston—

   Boston 19 Philadelphia 10

Philadelphia	0 2 0 0 2 0 5 1 0	= 10
Boston	11 0 3 0 0 5 0 0 X	= 19

6. May 6, 1934, at Boston—

Boston 14 Detroit 4

Detroit	2 0 0 0 0 0 0 1 1 = 4
Boston	0 1 0 12 1 0 0 0 X = 14

7. July 5, 1936, at Boston—

Boston 16 Philadelphia 2 (1st game)

Philadelphia	0 0 0 2 0 0 0 0 0 = 2
Boston	0 11 0 0 1 2 2 0 X = 16

8. July 25, 1936, at Detroit—

Boston 18 Detroit 3

Boston	0 6 0 0 12 0 0 0 0 = 18
Detroit	0 0 1 2 0 0 0 0 0 = 3

9. September 21, 1937, at Boston—

Boston 12 Detroit 7 (1st game)

Detroit	0 0 1 0 0 2 3 0 1 = 7
Boston	0 1 0 0 10 1 0 0 X = 12

10. August 25, 1940, at Boston—

Boston 17 St. Louis 3 (2nd game)

St. Louis	2 0 0 0 0 0 1 = 3
Boston	3 0 1 1 0 11 1 = 17

(Game called after seven innings)

11. September 27, 1940 at Boston—

Boston 24 Washington 4

Washington	2 0 0 0 0 0 2 0 0 = 4
Boston	1 0 5 10 1 0 0 7 X = 24

12. August 4, 1945, at Washington—

Boston 15 Washington 4 (2nd game)

Boston	1 0 1 12 0 1 0 0 0 = 15
Washington	0 1 1 0 0 1 0 0 1 = 4

13. July 4, 1948, at Boston—

Boston 19 Philadelphia 5

Philadelphia	0 0 0 0 0 3 2 0 0 = 5
Boston	0 1 0 0 1 3 14 0 X = 19

14. July 26, 1949, at Boston—

Boston 11 Chicago 2

Chicago	0 0 0 0 0 0 0 0 2 = 2
Boston	0 0 0 0 0 1 0 10 X = 11

15. April 30, 1950, at Boston—

Boston 19 Philadelphia 0 (1st game)

Philadelphia	0 0 0 0 0 0 0 0 0 = 0
Boston	4 3 0 11 0 0 0 1 X = 19

16. July 14, 1950, at Boston—

Boston 13 Chicago 1

Chicago	0 0 1 0 0 0 0 0 0 = 1
Boston	0 1 11 0 0 1 0 0 X = 13

17. June 23, 1952, at Detroit—

Boston 12 Detroit 6

Boston	0 0 1 11 0 0 0 0 0 = 12
Detroit	0 1 0 1 0 0 0 2 2 = 6

18. June 18, 1953, at Boston—

Boston 23 Detroit 3

Detroit	0 0 0 2 0 1 0 0 0 = 3
Boston	0 3 0 0 0 2 17 1 X = 23

19. August 26, 1957, at Kansas City—

Boston 16 Kansas City 0

Boston	2 1 1 0 0 0 10 1 1 = 16
Kansas City	0 0 0 0 0 0 0 0 0 = 0

20. May 4, 1962, at Boston—

Boston 13 Chicago 6

Chicago	0 1 0 3 0 1 1 0 0	= 6
Boston	0 0 0 0 12 0 1 0 X	= 13

21. August 10, 1965, at Boston—

Boston 15 Baltimore 5 (1st game)

Baltimore	0 0 3 1 0 0 0 0 1	= 5
Boston	0 1 1 0 12 1 0 0 X	= 15

22. June 8, 1977, at Boston—

Boston 14 Baltimore 5

Baltimore	0 1 0 0 0 0 0 4 0	= 5
Boston	0 1 1 3 0 0 0 0 X	= 14

23. August 21, 1986, at Cleveland—

Boston 24 Cleveland 5

Boston	0 0 4 2 0 12 1 5 0	= 24
Cleveland	1 0 0 0 0 0 1 0 3	= 5

24. July 30, 1991, at Boston—

Boston 11 Texas 6

Texas	0 1 1 0 0 0 2 2 0	= 6
Boston	0 1 1 10 0 0 0 0 X	= 11

Passed Ball Leaders

National League

1876	John Clapp	St. Louis	52
1877	Pop Snyder	Louisville	58
1878	Bill Harbidge	Chicago	56
1879	Charlie Reilly	Troy	89
1880	Emil Gross	Providence	73
1881	Pop Snyder	Boston	99
1882	Fatty Briody	Cleveland	70
1883	Mike Hines	Boston	99
1884	Doc Bushong	Cleveland	95
1885	George Myers	Buffalo	57
1886	Frank Graves	St. Louis	81
1887	Connie Mack	Washington	76
1888	Buck Ewing	New York	65
1889	Chief Zimmer	Cleveland	50
1890	Chief Zimmer	Cleveland	55
1891	Jerry Harrington	Cincinnati	36
1892	Jack Boyle	New York	71
1893	John Grim	Louisville	28
	Harry Vaughn	Cincinnati	28
1894	Duke Farrell	New York	34
1895	Deacon McGuire	Washington	28
1896	Marty Bergen	Boston	27
1897	Bill Wilson	Louisville	32
1898	Marty Bergen	Boston	38
1899	John Warner	New York	21
1900	Klondike Douglass	Philadelphia	27

Year	Player	Team	
1901	Frank Bowerman	New York	21
1902	Johnny Kling	Chicago	17
1903	Pat Moran	Boston	24
1904	Johnny Kling	Chicago	16
	Tom Needham	Boston	16
1905	Pat Moran	Boston	22
1906	Roger Bresnahan	New York	16
1907	Red Dooin	Philadelphia	16
1908	Roger Bresnahan	New York	17
1909	Red Dooin	Philadelphia	15
	Peaches Graham	Boston	15
1910	Chief Meyers	New York	17
1911	Johnny Kling	Chicago-Boston	13
1912	George Gibson	Pittsburgh	12
	Chief Meyers	New York	12
1913	Mike Simon	Pittsburgh	9
1914	Jimmy Archer	Chicago	16
1915	Jimmy Archer	Chicago	14
1916	Ed Burns	Philadelphia	14
	Ivey Wingo	Cincinnati	14
1917	Ivey Wingo	Cincinnati	16
1918	Mike Gonzalez	St. Louis	8
1919	Ivey Wingo	Cincinnati	11
	Ernie Krueger	Brooklyn	11
1920	Otto Miller	Brooklyn	13
1921	Otto Miller	Brooklyn	11
1922	Earl Smith	New York	11
1923	Zack Taylor	Brooklyn	13
1924	Gabby Hartnett	Chicago	12
1925	Jimmie Wilson	Philadelphia	9
	Zack Taylor	Brooklyn	9
	Bubbles Hargrave	Cincinnati	9
	Earl Smith	Pittsburgh	9
1926	Zack Taylor	Boston	13
1927	Gabby Hartnett	Chicago	12
1928	Zack Taylor	Boston	11
1929	Val Picinich	Brooklyn	9
1930	Gabby Hartnett	Chicago	10
1931	Rollie Hemsley	Pittsburgh-Chicago	9
1932	Ernie Lombardi	Cincinnati	17
1933	Gus Mancuso	New York	12
1934	Gus Mancuso	New York	11
1935	Ernie Lombardi	Cincinnati	10
1936	Ernie Lombardi	Cincinnati	7
	Ray Berres	Brooklyn	7
1937	Ernie Lombardi	Cincinnati	13
1938	Ernie Lombardi	Cincinnati	9
1939	Ernie Lombardi	Cincinnati	15
1940	Ernie Lombardi	Cincinnati	7
	Bennie Warren	Philadelphia	7
	Harry Danning	New York	7
1941	Ernie Lombardi	Cincinnati	16
1942	Ray Lamanno	Cincinnati	11
1943	Mickey Owen	Brooklyn	9
	Walker Cooper	St. Louis	9
1944	Mickey Owen	Brooklyn	11
1945	Ernie Lombardi	New York	9
1946	Ferrell Anderson	Brooklyn	9

1947	Andy Seminick	Philadelphia	17
1948	Ed Fitzgerald	Pittsburgh	15
1949	Walker Cooper	New York-Cincinnati	15
1950	Johnny Pramesa	Cincinnati	11
1951	Joe Garagiola	St. Louis-Pittsburgh	9
1952	Wes Westrum	New York	13
1953	Mike Sandlock	Pittsburgh	15
1954	Ray Katt	New York	12
1955	Ray Katt	New York	17
	Harry Chiti	Chicago	17
1956	Wes Westrum	New York	13
1957	Cal Neeman	Chicago	13
1958	Bob Schmidt	San Francisco	10
1959	Del Crandall	Milwaukee	15
1960	John Roseboro	Los Angeles	10
1961	Dick Bertell	Chicago	23
1962	Johnny Edwards	Cincinnati	16
	Dick Bertell	Chicago	16
	Clay Dalrymple	Philadelphia	16
1963	John Bateman	Houston	16
	Tim McCarver	St. Louis	16
1964	Jesse Gonder	New York	21
1965	Tim McCarver	St. Louis	18
1966	John Bateman	Houston	21
1967	Bob Uecker	Philadelphia-Atlanta	27
1968	Johnny Bench	Cincinnati	18
1969	Bob Didier	Atlanta	27
1970	Dick Dietz	San Francisco	25
1971	Dick Dietz	San Francisco	20
1972	Earl Williams	Atlanta	28
1973	Ted Simmons	St. Louis	25
1974	Johnny Oates	Atlanta	15
1975	Ted Simmons	St. Louis	28
1976	Cliff Johnson	Houston	12
1977	Joe Ferguson	Houston	16
1978	Joe Nolan	Atlanta	14
1979	Ted Simmons	St. Louis	14
1980	Alan Ashby	Houston	14
1981	Mike Scioscia	Los Angeles	11
1982	Luis Pujols	Houston	20
1983	Jody Davis	Chicago	21
1984	Mark Bailey	Houston	18
1985	Mark Bailey	Houston	19
1986	John Russell	Philadelphia	17
1987	Benito Santiago	San Diego	22
1988	Lance Parrish	Philadelphia	12
1989	Benito Santiago	San Diego	14
1990	Joe Girardi	Chicago	16
	Joe Oliver	Cincinnati	16
1991	Craig Biggio	Houston	13
1992	Mike Scioscia	Los Angeles	14

Passed Ball Leaders

American League

1901	Mike Powers	Philadelphia	19
1902	Harry Bemis	Cleveland	22
1903	Fred Abbott	Cleveland	17
1904	Fritz Buelow	Detroit-Cleveland	14
1905	Lou Criger	Boston	13
	Nig Clarke	Cleveland-Detroit	13
1906	Red Kleinow	New York	14
1907	Nig Clarke	Cleveland	25
1908	Lou Criger	Boston	14
1909	Gabby Street	Washington	15
1910	Bill Carrigan	Boston	15
1911	John Henry	Washington	25
1912	Oscar Stanage	Detroit	17
1913	Jeff Sweeney	New York	19
1914	Sam Agnew	St. Louis	18
1915	Sam Agnew	St. Louis	17
1916	John Henry	Washington	18
1917	Hank Severeid	St. Louis	19
1918	Eddie Ainsmith	Washington	13
1919	Wally Schang	Boston	14
1920	Cy Perkins	Philadelphia	12
1921	Cy Perkins	Philadelphia	12
1922	Steve O'Neill	Cleveland	17
1923	Cy Perkins	Philadelphia	16
1924	Steve O'Neill	Boston	14
1925	Mickey Cochrane	Philadelphia	12
1926	Mickey Cochrane	Philadelphia	8
1927	Wally Schang	St. Louis	9
1928	Luke Sewell	Cleveland	13
1929	Mickey Cochrane	Philadelphia	9
	Luke Sewell	Cleveland	9
1930	Ray Hayworth	Detroit	11
1931	Mickey Cochrane	Philadelphia	6
	Rick Ferrell	St. Louis	6
	Charlie Berry	Boston	6
1932	Mickey Cochrane	Philadelphia	11
1933	Bill Dickey	New York	10
1934	Ed Madjeski	Philadelphia-Chicago	9
1935	Luke Sewell	Chicago	9
	Cliff Bolton	Washington	9
1936	Frankie Hayes	Philadelphia	17
1937	Rudy York	Detroit	12
1938	Frankie Hayes	Philadelphia	10
	Rudy York	Detroit	10
1939	Rick Ferrell	Washington	19
1940	Rick Ferrell	Washington	17
1941	Jake Early	Washington	17
1942	Hal Wagner	Philadelphia	15
1943	Jake Early	Washington	13
	Hal Wagner	Philadelphia	13
1944	Rick Ferrell	Washington	20
1945	Rick Ferrell	Washington	21
1946	Al Evans	Washington	18
1947	George Dickey	Chicago	8

1948	Bob Swift	Detroit	10		1974	Fran Healy	Kansas City	21
1949	Mickey Guerra	Philadelphia	7		1975	Darrell Porter	Milwaukee	15
1950	Yogi Berra	New York	7		1976	Thurman Munson	New York	12
1951	Matt Batts	Boston-St. Louis	11			Darrell Porter	Milwaukee	12
1952	Clint Courtney	St. Louis	11		1977	Charlie Moore	Milwaukee	14
1953	Matt Batts	Detroit	13		1978	Darrell Porter	Kansas City	9
1954	Sammy White	Boston	11		1979	Lance Parrish	Detroit	21
1955	Hal Smith	Baltimore	14		1980	Jim Sundberg	Texas	14
1956	Tim Thompson	Kansas City	9			Lance Parrish	Detroit	14
1957	Hal Smith	Kansas City	16		1981	Jim Sundberg	Texas	8
1958	Harry Chiti	Kansas City	18		1982	Jim Sundberg	Texas	16
1959	Gus Triandos	Baltimore	28		1983	Carlton Fisk	Chicago	11
1960	Earl Battey	Washington	18		1984	Donnie Scott	Texas	18
1961	Gus Triandos	Baltimore	21		1985	Ron Hassey	New York	15
1962	John Romano	Cleveland	15		1986	Rich Gedman	Boston	14
1963	Gus Triandos	Detroit	14		1987	Gino Petralli	Texas	35
1964	J. C. Martin	Chicago	24		1988	Gino Petralli	Texas	20
1965	J. C. Martin	Chicago	33		1989	Chad Kreuter	Texas	21
1966	Andy Etchebarren	Baltimore	15		1990	Gino Petralli	Texas	20
1967	Jose Azcue	Cleveland	17		1991	Lance Parrish	California	19
1968	Duke Sims	Cleveland	13		1992	Brian Harper	Minnesota	12
	Russ Gibson	Boston	13					
1969	Ed Herrmann	Chicago	19					
1970	Jose Azcue	California	17					
	Ray Fosse	Cleveland	17					
1971	Ed Herrmann	Chicago	16					
	Dick Billings	Washington	16					
1972	Ed Hermann	Chicago	18					
1973	Ed Hermann	Chicago	24					

Passed Ball Leaders

American Association

1882	Ed Whiting	Baltimore	105
1883	Jackie Hayes	Pittsburgh	93
1884	Fleet Walker	Toledo	72
1885	Bill Traffley	Baltimore	104
1886	Fred Carroll	Pittsburgh	95
1887	Wilbert Robinson	Philadelphia	82
1888	Pop Snyder	Cleveland	57
1889	Paul Cook	Louisville	77
1890	Jack O'Connor	Columbus	58
1891	Jocko Milligan	Philadelphia	40

Passed Ball Leaders

Union Association

1884	Eddie Fusselback	Baltimore	74

Passed Ball Leaders

Players' League

1890	Sy Sutcliffe	Cleveland	55

Passed Ball Leaders

Federal League

1914	Ted Easterly	Kansas City	17
1915	Grover Hartley	St. Louis	17

This is a list of twentieth century catchers who had a minimum of 100 passed balls.

Catcher	Years Played	Passed Balls
Ted Simmons	1968-1988	182
Lance Parrish*	1977-1992	173
Steve O'Neill	1911-1925, 1927-1928	145
Ernie Lombardi	1931-1947	143
Red Dooin	1902-1916	142
Rick Ferrell	1929-1945, 1947	142
Frankie Hayes	1933-1947	139
Gus Triandos	1953-1965	138
Tim McCarver	1959-1961, 1963-1980	132
Darrell Porter	1971-1987	132
Wally Schang	1913-1931	131
Jim Sundberg	1974-1989	130
Roger Bresnahan	1897, 1900-1915	129
Carlton Fisk*	1969, 1971-1992	127
Johnny Kling	1900-1908, 1910-1913	126
Gabby Hartnett	1922-1941	126
Ed Herrmann	1967, 1969-1978	125
J.C. Martin	1959-1972	121

Tom Haller	1961-1972	121
John Roseboro	1957-1970	113
Alan Ashby	1973-1989	113
Bill Freehan	1961, 1963-1976	106
John Bateman	1963-1972	104
Johnny Edwards	1961-1974	102
George Gibson	1905-1918	101
Oscar Stanage	1906, 1909-1920, 1925	100

(*) Still Active

Many catchers who played primarily in the nineteenth century had more than 200 passed balls. The three all-time leaders are:

Pop Snyder	1876-1879, 1881-1891	647
Silver Flint	1878-1889	602
Doc Bushong	1876, 1880-1890	553

For more than twenty years, the Society for American Baseball Research has published unique, insightful, entertaining literature. In addition to SABR's annual publications, Baseball Research Journal and The National Pastime, special issues have focused on specific aspects of baseball history. For further reading enjoyment, consider obtaining the SABR publications below.

PUBLICATIONS ORDER FORM

Baseball Research Journals

_____ 1975 (112 pp.) $3.00
_____ 1976 (128 pp.) $4.00
_____ 1977 (144 pp.) $4.00
_____ 1978 (160 pp.) $4.00
_____ 1979 (160 pp.) $5.00
_____ 1980 (180 pp.) $5.00
_____ 1981 (180 pp.) $5.00
  * 1982 (184 pp.) $5.00
  * 1983 (188 pp.) $5.00
_____ 1984 (88 pp.) $6.00
_____ 1985 (88 pp.) $6.00
_____ 1986 (88 pp.) $6.00
_____ 1987 (88 pp.) $6.00
_____ 1988 (88 pp.) $7.00
_____ 1989 (88 pp.) $8.00
_____ 1990 (96 pp.) $8.00
_____ 1991 (96 pp.) $8.00
_____ 1992 (96 pp.) $7.95

Baseball Historical Review

_____ 1981; Best of '72-'74
        Baseball Research Journals $6.00

Index to SABR Publications

_____ 1987 (58 pp.) $3.00
        The National Pastime,
        Baseball Research Journal,
        & SABR Review of Books

The Baseball Research Handbook

_____ 1987 (120 pp.) $6.00
        How to Do Research

The National Pastime

_____ #1: Fall, 1982 (88 pp.) $5.00
  * #2: Fall, 1983 (88 pp.) $5.00
_____ #3: Spring, 1984 (88 pp.) $7.00
        19th Century Pictorial
_____ #4: Spring, 1985 (88 pp.) $6.00
_____ #5: Winter, 1985 (88 pp.) $6.00
_____ #6: Spring, 1986 (88 pp.) $8.00
        Dead Ball Era Pictorial
_____ #7: Winter, 1987 (88 pp.) $6.00
_____ #8: Spring, 1988 (80 pp.) $8.00
        Nap Lajoie Biography
  * #9: 1989 (88 pp.) .... $ 8.00
        The Big Bang Era Pictorial
_____ #10: Fall, 1990 (88 pp.) $8.00
_____ #11: Fall, 1991 (88 pp.) $7.95
_____ #12: Summer, 1992 (96 pp.) . $7.95
        The International Pastime

19th Century Stars

_____ 1988 (144 pp.) $10.00
        Biographies of America's First Heroes
        (Non-Hall of Fame players)

Baseball in the 19th Century

_____ 1986; An Overview $2.00

The Federal League of 1914-15

_____ 1989 (64 pp.) $12.00
        Baseball's Third Major League

Award Voting

_____ 1988 (72 pp.) $7.00
        History & Listing of MVP, Rookie of
        the Year & Cy Young Awards

Cooperstown Corner

Columns from The Sporting News by Lee Allen
_____ 1990 (181 pp.) $10.00

SABR Review of Books

Articles of Baseball Literary Criticism
_____ Vol. I, 1986 .... $6.00
_____ Vol. II, 1987 (96 pp.) $6.00
_____ Vol. III, 1988 (104 pp.) $6.00
_____ Vol. IV, 1989 (128 pp.) $7.00
_____ Vol. V, 1990 (148 pp.) $7.00

Baseball in Cleveland

  * 1990 (40 pp.) $7.50

Baseball in New York

_____ 1991 (36 pp.) $5.00

St. Louis's Favorite Sport

_____ 1992 (64 pp.) $7.50

Minor League Baseball Stars

_____ Vol. I, 1978 (132 pp.) $5.00
        Year-by-year records of
        170 minor league greats
_____ Vol. II, 1984 .... $5.00
        20 managers and 180 more players
_____ Vol. III, 1992 .... $9.95
        250 players

Minor League History Journal

_____ 1991 (40 pp.) $6.00
        Stories and statistics

Run, Rabbit, Run

_____ 1991 (96 pp.) $9.95
        Tales of Walter "Rabbit" Maranville

Baseball: The Fan's Game (reprint)

_____ by Mickey Cochrane (189 pp.) $9.95

* = Out of Print.

SABR members receive Baseball Research Journal, The National Pastime, one or more special publications, membership directory, and The SABR Bulletin, SABR's monthly newsletter. Additional membership benefits include access to a national convention and regional meetings, research exchange and research paper collection, the SABR lending library, and nearly six thousand baseball enthusiasts like yourself around the country and the world. You are welcome to join any of SABR's 14 research committees.

To join SABR (membership dues are $35 U.S., $45 Canada & Mexico, $50 elsewhere) send check or money order (U.S. funds only) to: SABR, P.O. Box 93183, Cleveland, OH 44101.

SHIPPING & HANDLING

Please add $1.50 for 1 book, $2.50 for 2 or 3 books, and $5.00 when ordering 4 or 5 books. For more than 5 books, add $.50 per book. Ohio residents, add 7% sales tax. Foreign delivery, add an additional $1.00 in each category.

Make checks payable to:

SABR, P.O. Box 93183
Cleveland, OH 44101.

S H I P T O		
Name _____		
Address _____		
City, State, ZIP _____		

Here's
The Pitch

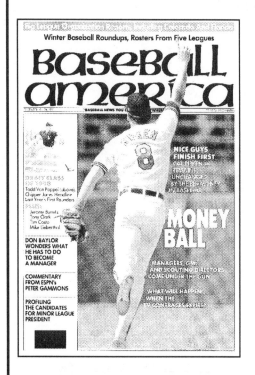

Pencil Yourself Into The Lineup. Don't Get Caught Looking.

We take the mound 26 times a year. And as a 12-year veteran, we've developed quite a repertoire. We paint the corners with our special reports and insightful examinations of trends of the game.

Our colorful features, both major and minor league, will entice you like a lollipop curve. Our draft coverage and prospect lists are nothing but heat, right down the middle. And we may surprise you with an occasional knuckleball, just a tinge of humor and irreverence that helps weave the fabric of baseball.

We blaze the trail for you to follow your favorite prospects up the ladder to stardom, with complete minor league statistics and reports. And even before they sign their first professional contract, we've got our eye on them with college and amateur news.

From Lynchburg to Pittsburgh, Tokyo to Omaha, **Baseball America** keeps you in touch with the game.

And, If you subscribe now, we'll include as a FREE GIFT our 1993 Almanac, a $12.95 value which you'll refer to for years to come.

BaseBall
america™

"BASEBALL NEWS YOU CAN'T GET ANYWHERE ELSE"
BASEBALL AMERICA · P.O. BOX 2089 · DURHAM, NC 27702 · 1-800-845-2726